Blame it on fast foods

By

B. J. T. Pepin

Ostrich Canada

First Edition

Edited and published by: Ostrich Canada, Barrie, Ontario

For information about this publication or Ostrich Canada's services, make contact via the following website: www.ostrichcanada.ca

Library and Archives Canada Cataloguing in Publication

Pepin, B. J. T., 1960-, author
    Blame it on fast foods / by B.J.T. Pepin.

Issued in print and electronic formats.
ISBN 978-0-9881055-0-8 (pbk.).--ISBN 978-0-9881055-1-5 (epub)

    1. Canadian wit and humor (English). 2. Convenience foods--Humor. 3. Conduct of life--Humor. I. Title.

PS8631.E62B53 2013   C818'.602   C2013-908039-2
                                               C2013-908040-6

Dedication

I believe that giving recognition underlines the important contributions that people make in so many ways, even though they may not be aware of the role they've played.

First, I thank my wife. She has put up with many moves, absences, and constant demands brought on by life associated with the Armed Forces. She continues to be the proverbial "rock" in my life, providing a firm foundation that has allowed me to "do my thing." She's been there through thick and thin, and in times when I've had to heal from some of the insane stunts I've pulled over the years. She is living proof of the significance of unconditional love.

Second, I thank my parents. Although they may not know, they have taught me what parenting is all about. They are true examples of how we should go about living and overcoming challenges that you wouldn't wish on your worst enemies.

Third, I thank my kids. They have been examples of flexibility and adaptability in many trying situations. And I thank them for providing me with beautiful grandchildren, thus allowing me to live on in blood.

Fourth, I thank my brothers. They too have had their fair share of challenges and have shown great resiliency in overcoming difficult circumstances.

And last, I thank the service members who sacrifice so much for their countries, as well as their families for the support they give and sacrifices they too must make.

Acknowledgements

Special thanks are in order to Steve who spawned the idea for this book and came up with the title. Actually, I hope this is kept in mind if a fast-food chain considers taking legal action against anyone. If anyone is upset by what I have to say, I'll be more than happy to pass on Steve's contact information!

Preface

What are you doing reading a book like this? The only thing you'll get out of it is a skewed view of what we've become in this Western society that we all seem to cherish so much.

I don't profess to be an expert of any kind. I won't try to convince you of how to go about changing your life. I won't present you with a step-by-step process to right the wrongs in your life or the lives of those who are close to you. Don't expect to find any gems of wisdom or pearls of great price.

You won't find any quotes, references, footnotes, stats from experts, or any of that kind of stuff. I may make reference to some past news items, but that's about it. And if ever you think that I've plagiarized anyone, you've spent more time looking into the details than you needed to. All of this is my own—a barebones, no-holds-barred perspective on what our lives have become.

So, what will come of you after reading this book? To be honest, I have no idea! Take what you want, leave what you will. And if you want to debate any subject, contact Steve—I'm sure he'd be more than happy to speak with you. Be sure to leave him a tip, though—he'd love the extra income!

Contents

CHAPTER ONE

Life and Fast-Food Restaurants

Let's start by asking two simple questions: What is a "fast-food restaurant"? And why are they so popular?

At a fast-food restaurant, you pay someone money to make you a meal right then and there. In the whole transaction, you barely need to lift a finger to have your food prepared. Sounds great, doesn't it?

Given our inherent laziness, this kind of service definitely meets our need to be served on hand and foot. It's no wonder why fast-food restaurants have increased in popularity over the years…hand in hand with an increase in obesity rates. But I digress…

And talking about their popularity, it makes me wonder: Is it possible that the fast-food chains have put some sort of ingredient into the food to make us keep eating it? If you think about it, there very well could be an addictive component within the junk.

Actually, when we eat fast foods, we're often eating products that are barely fit for human consumption. Do you really know what the fast-food chains are serving you? Do you really believe the pamphlets detailing the contents of the food? What's *really* in the food? Outside of dependency-creating ingredients, maybe they're literally recycling the world's garbage by adding it to the junk. Wouldn't that be the ultimate insult?!

And further on that note, have you ever considered the possibility that there's a conspiracy to make every Westerner obese and sick so the medical system can justify its existence? Might the fast-food business simply be a money-making racket for the medical and insurance heavyweights?

Imagine this: If we didn't go to fast-food joints, we just might be healthier. And if we were healthier, it would greatly reduce the demands on the health care system, in turn increasing the quality of care.

What the government and medical systems aren't telling us is that the poor quality of care is actually a plan designed to exterminate the members of our society unfortunate enough to have chosen to consume unhealthy food—the ones offered at fast-food chains. Remember Darwin and his belief of "survival of the fittest"?

Each time you eat fast food, the negative effects compound, in turn shortening your life expectancy. So, when all's said and done, those folks who frequent fast-food joints wind up paying a much steeper price than they think they do; the cost of eating a hamburger is much greater than the $5.99 you fork out to the cashier.

Back on the topic of our inherent laziness, at a fast-food restaurant, the meal is typically in your stomach about ten minutes after you've ordered it—and that's when the restaurant is busy! I wonder which came first: our need for instant gratification, or did the fast-food restaurants create the need? Maybe it's part of their conspiracy to create dependence within the populace; by influencing us to buy more fast food, the fast-food chains are able to rake in the bucks, in turn allowing them to pay off government officials so the cycle can continue.

It's come to the point where we, as a people, want everything yesterday. It's the exact opposite of what health experts are drilling into us regarding stress; we're constantly being told to slow down, yet we have a tendency to go to fast-food joints to speed things up. Strange, isn't it? We're being manipulated to the extreme! The fast-food conglomerates created the need and maintain it in us as well!

For me, personally, my involvement with fast foods has brought about some near death experiences. Think about it: You're in so much of a hurry that you gobble down the food so fast that you end up choking half to death! Isn't going to a fast-food restaurant supposed to allow you to relax and save time that would have otherwise been spent preparing a meal? But how many of us actually take advantage of this? Instead, we wind up wolfing everything down and hurrying to the next pressing matter. We don't even give ourselves the time to catch our own breaths!

And then there are the families that go out to fast-food restaurants to spend quality time with each other. Does this usually happen? Nope! Instead, we turn out sending the children off to be babysat by some plastic, toy-filled play land while we parents sit back and inhale our food. Is this quality family time or what?! Indeed, some would argue that we bring our children to fast-food restaurants to meet their need for fun and excitement. For sure we do—there's nothing more fun and exciting than eating your way to obesity!

Of all the reasons why we go to fast-food restaurants, none of them are any good. The junk that we consume is horrible for us both mentally and physically, before, during, and after we eat it. Really, fast-food restaurants are bad for society in general. Throughout the rest of this book, I'm going to give you some reasons why...and why you should blame it all on fast foods.

CHAPTER TWO

Business and Work

Our society revolves around the consumption of goods and services. Basically, what this means is that we exist to use things and each other. In life, the better you are at using things and other people, the further you will get ahead. Disagree? Just look to the world of business.

Show me any executive or official and I'll show you a trail of pain and suffering endured by the many who have been in contact with the individual. Most, if not all, of them have back-stabbed, stepped on, lied to, brushed aside, ignored, laughed at, laid off, fired, accused, stole credit from, screwed (literally and figuratively), kept information from, used, took advantage of, and abused someone on their way to the top. Sure, some might have been "nice" about it while others were cut-throat, but they're all the same. I mean, I couldn't say for a fact that all high-ranking people have acted in such a manner, but I believe I can safely say that those who haven't are an exception to the rule.

And now that I've spoken negatively about practically every rich and powerful person out there (whoops!), let's get back to my comment about how our society revolves around the consumption of goods and services...

When I speak about consumption, I mean exactly what I say: We live to consume and we consume to live. By definition, the word "consume" means: to destroy by separating the component parts and annihilating the form of the substance, as by fire or eating; to destroy by dissipating or by use; to expend; to waste; to spend; to pass (time); to waste slowly; to bring to ruin. To that, all I can say is, "Wow." Does this say it all or what?!

Business and Work

If you take the time to think about it, everything we do is based on consumption—destroying things; annihilation; expending; wasting. So, what does that make each and every one of us? We're all consumers—those who destroy, annihilate, expend, and waste. This is especially true for us who live in the Western world. Some call it "free enterprise" or "capitalism." But what is consumption really all about? As I alluded to at the start of this chapter, it's all about greed.

We are more or less stuck, having to operate in the hustle and bustle world to make ends meet—the proverbial "rat race." On a side note, how fitting of a saying given that we—especially us who are most greedy—perpetuate the cycle of consumption in hope of getting somewhere. Like a hamster on a wheel, we simply go 'round in circles, going nowhere fast and using up a lot of energy in the process.

For me, I prefer the aboriginals' approach to matters—the "I'll get there when the time is right" approach. If we all lived more like this, it would surely reduce the amount of stress that we encounter on a daily basis. We'd be a heck of a lot more healthy, that's for sure! But we're too greedy to slow things down, just like the fast-food conglomerates.

Many would say that we all have a choice in this. But, in my opinion, we don't; unless you want to live like a hermit in the middle of nowhere and cut yourself off from the rest of the world, you have no choice but to consume just like everyone else. So, instead, what can you do? Blame it on fast foods!

CHAPTER THREE

Finances

As the rich are stepping on others to get richer, everyone else—the "regular Joes"—must scrape by to make ends meet. With the ever-changing tides that the financial world brings, all non-executives live and work under a constant fear of lay-offs, downsizing, or outright closures. And in addition to concerns related to job security, there's the ongoing expenses we have no choice but to pay—food, clothing, housing, transportation, and the like—all while making mere pennies for our hard work. But these expenses are just a fraction of the price we have to pay to live in this capitalistic society…

In everyday life, we can't help but compare what we own to the possessions of others. We think in terms of what they have and what we don't. And when they have something we don't have, we become jealous pretty darn quick! We think: "It's not fair for them to have 'this' or 'that' when we don't!" Everyone is constantly trying to "keep up with the Joneses" next door. So, it all comes back to pride and greed.

And where did this type of mindset come from? As far as I'm concerned, it has existed since the beginning of time. For those of you who believe in The Bible, I submit the story of Cane and Able. If you don't know it already, long story short, Cane murders Able.

Anyway, both ancient and modern pundits have typically supposed that Cane's actions were driven by jealousy since God rejected his offerings and accepted Abel's. Some suggest even more, stating that the motive involved a desire for the most beautiful woman. So, you see what I mean about pride and greed?

Now, what causes our pride and greed? Yes, you guessed it: Power! And in this society, how do we get power? You got it: Money!

Don't go and lie to me, or most importantly yourself—everyone wants money. Everyone wants more of it. In the Western world, it's an obsession. And what is the result? Many will kill for money!

However, in the grand scheme of things, no matter how much money we accumulate, we never truly have any. Why? Because the massive corporations own all of it—heck, they own all of us consumers for that matter. They control our lives by dictating what we want and need and what we have to do to get it. They dictate how much we pay for everything. It's all part of an ultimate and unavoidable truth, and here is why it'll never go away…

Many of us think free enterprise reigns and that the government plays a significant role in monitoring and establishing parameters associated with quality and sales. But, in reality, it's the opposite; since corporations own everything, they have their thumbs on all facets of society, including the government. They have control over everything and everyone! You've seen it for yourself: Massive corporations have our "leaders" so deep in their back pockets that the government thinks the corporations are "the people." Don't believe me? Just look at where government officials go after retiring from the public sector: Right to an executive position with one of the conglomerates.

Blame it on fast foods

So, you're probably asking: "What can we do about it?" "What can we do to turn the tide and regain control over our countries and our lives?" Well, I'm afraid that there isn't much we can do, short of us all rebelling together simultaneously... Actually, that's it! We need a revolution! But fat chance that'll ever happen. Instead, we should all settle on doing what I do: Blame it on fast foods!

CHAPTER FOUR

Sports

There is no denying that sport is big business. And because of how much money there is tied into sport, it can't help but attract unsavory characters. Although some might argue that it's a leap to associate sport with fast food or vice versa, there's a definite relationship. In this world, wherever there's money, the fast-food industry is present.

Being involved in sport allows fast-food companies to exercise control over athletes, venues, and fans alike. They fork out bucket loads of cash to endorse athletes whose star status influences the populace to buy more burgers, fries, and "sugar water." They have a stranglehold on the revenue of venues from their restaurants, spatter every surface with advertisements, and get a "plug" each time the announcer has something to say on the loudspeaker. Meanwhile, fans sit at the events for hours, exposed to this barrage of publicities that impact every one of their senses. And on the topic of how long the events are, have you ever wondered if they make them long on purpose so people get hungry while they're there? It's tough not to eat something if the whole outing lasts six hours from start to finish…

But anyway, let's go back to a comment I made in the first chapter about how everyone has gotten used to getting everything they want right away, without having to lift more than a finger. Being raised with that as your reality, think about what would happen if you became a top athlete. Not only would you have the money to get whatever you want whenever you want it, but people would bend over backwards to please you just because you're famous.

Blame it on fast foods

Basically, when you become a star athlete, your whole life becomes the equivalent of a fast-food restaurant. You accidentally dropped your phone in a puddle? Your sponsor will send you a new one that day. You don't like the suede seats in your sports car? They'll take back the whole car and make you a new one. And if you ever get hungry, you'll have a limo outside your house in minutes, sent by your fast-food sponsor to bring you back into their arms. You get all of this and all you have to do in return is smile for the camera and say, "This is the juiciest burger I've ever eaten!"

With this kind of lifestyle, it's no wonder why some athletes have gotten into addictions and other trouble. They get that big, fat contract and forget that they're still meant to work for the things they receive. But after a while, some athletes get so used to being waited on hand and foot that they forget how they became a professional athlete in the first place; they have to remember: Life is not a fast-food restaurant.

In the end, team owners are greedy, trying to make all of the money they can from sponsors while squeezing their fans for every penny they possess. Fans want winning teams year after year without exception. And athletes, they want everything and more just to play a game.

Where does this all come from? In my opinion, it's our far-reaching need to get everything right here, right now—the fast-food mentality. And who's to blame for this shameful and unshakable character trait that we've all inherited? Blame it on fast foods!

CHAPTER FIVE

Entertainment

As there is in the sports industry, there's big money in entertainment. New movies, TV series, music concerts, albums, and more are pumped out every minute. They're all force-fed to us everywhere we go—a new romantic comedy with "Heartthrob Guy" falling for "Awkward yet Cute Girl"; be sure to check out the new TV series on "Real Live People with Strange Obsessions"; and "Johnny Guitar-Player" came out with his new teenage rebellion album—and oh, you need it! It's embarrassing the amount of garbage that gets put in front of us!

Actually, when you think about it, with the volume and frequency of "new and exciting entertainment," it's no wonder why so many kids are getting diagnosed with ADHD. Nowadays, parents are too busy working two jobs and planning their next divorce to spend any time with their children. Instead, they just throw dinner in the microwave, turn on the TV, and gently nudge their kids towards the couch. Oh the love! But more on relationships and parenting later...

Besides the fact that new shows come at us every 30 minutes, take a look at the structure of TV shows and movies. TV shows never run for longer than three scenes over the span of six minutes before viewers are stuck watching ads about how they can "defeat acne like 'Ms. Teenage Supermodel' if they just use this special potion." And it's no different at the movie theatre—they schedule films to start at such and such time, yet the first 15 minutes are made up of nothing but advertisements. It's brutal!

Blame it on fast foods

Likewise, have you noticed the advertisements placed within TV shows and movies? Both of them are packed with subliminal messages—each and every scene involves the characters eating or drinking some sort of name-brand item! Now you know why you suddenly have a craving to go into your pantry to get a bag of chips, or why you want to drive to the fast-food joint down the street before the next show starts...

The reality is that it's all about the money. Besides the fact that the cost to be "entertained" is outrageous, there's the constant recycling of the same old themes and rereleases of past "classics" or best sellers. Well, guess what producers: The "remastered" version is still junk! It appears as though the craft of entertaining doesn't matter anymore. There are very few real artists out there these days—it's simply not profitable enough!

With the amount of entertainment that's produced, it's obvious that it's all about volume and profits. If you stop and think for a second, what does this remind you of? Yes, you know what I'm getting at... Who should you blame for this overabundance of cookie-cutter garbage that we consider entertainment? Blame it on fast foods!

CHAPTER SIX

Travel and Vacations

To be honest, all you need to do is drive in your car for two minutes to know where I'm going with this chapter. You know what it's like out there—the minute you're at the wheel and moving, you're taking your life in your own hands! Actually, I'd argue that you're putting it in others' hands, but you get what I mean.

Seriously though, what the heck is going on out there?! I swear, everyone should pop a Valium or two to bring themselves down a notch before hitting the road. No, scratch that—it'd probably make them even more dangerous! I don't know if I'm the only one who feels this way, but every time I'm out on the road, I feel closer to death. It's like accidents are just waiting to happen!

On the subject of drugs, some folks are addicted to speed, in this case referring to whizzing down the freeway at 100 miles per hour or more. When people get behind the wheel, they are overcome by the fact that they finally have control and power. But with a 2000 pound vehicle in their hands, these people can do some serious damage. This is especially true since they get this power when they're stressed-out and in a hurry. Talk about a dangerous situation!

So, what's the result? Roadside fistfights, accidents on purpose, and countless other examples of road rage. This makes it even more dangerous than it already is with things like bad weather and poor road conditions. Honestly, with all of these hazards, we're going to have to start driving around in armoured vehicles to stay safe! In no time, we'll start getting used to hearing: "Honey, did you remember to put the umbrella in the back of the tank?

And on that note, I turn towards one of our favourite pastimes: Vacation. When any holiday approaches, everything gets a lot more expensive—the price of gas goes up, flights cost more, and if you can find accommodations, they too cost an arm and a leg.

Then, to add to the fun, it seems like every last person has taken a vacation at the same time as you and at the same spot that you chose. I'm sure you've lived the result: Everyone hurries up to go nowhere fast; everyone gets on the road at the same time, going to the same place, and you wind up stuck in one gigantic parking lot. Is that a great start to a vacation or what?! Time after time, it's as if you lose half of your vacation just trying to get to the place that you were headed to.

And how about when you get to your destination? You think it's all over, but the whole story repeats itself—instead of being in boarding lineups, traffic jams, or otherwise, now you're in lineups for amusement park rides, to get a table at a restaurant, and for everything else you want to do. Then what happens? Everyone starts getting impatient and winds up stepping on and over each other trying to expedite the process. What ever happened to that much-needed break?! It's no wonder why people always say they need a vacation: They never turn out relaxing enough to have one!

What's the root cause of all this horror? The fast-food mentality of course! We're so stressed-out and in a hurry that we get into countless accidents and altercations over the course of our travels. And if you stop to think about it, both of these unfortunate events make the conglomerates money through insurance claims, lawsuits, and so on. It's as if they're purposely pushing us into a perpetual system of unsatisfying vacations, forcing us to take them again and again to try to satisfy our need for relaxation. Meanwhile, throughout our travels, we're eating at fast-food restaurants to get back all of the time we've wasted. They make it so you're dammed if you do and dammed if you don't! And what's the one and only thing that you can do about it all? You've got it: Blame it on fast foods!

CHAPTER SEVEN

Education

The fast-food mentality has infiltrated the educational system. Want proof? Look down the road to the nearest school—they've adopted the same conveyor-belt approach to teaching our children. And regretfully, it appears as though parents have bought into this system wholeheartedly, selling out their children—and our future—in the process.

Think about it: At a young and tender age, parents rip their children away from the safe and comfortable surroundings that the home has to offer…or supposedly safe and comfortable surroundings, but more on parenting later. Anyway, this exodus happens when kids are at the most impressionable stage of their lives. The children are discarded and thrown into schools where everyone must follow in single file, participate in the same activities, only take in what the teacher presents, and regurgitate what's been shoved down their throats. Altogether, each and every one of them is to think the same and do the same things with no room for "thinking outside of the box." Nope, you surely can't "have it your own way" in today's education system…

And by buying into this approach, what are we actually creating through education? With a process that's streamlined for efficiency's sake, we're producing a bunch of children bearing the same of everything. Do I hear the word "clone"?

Further on this thought, what picture do you have in your mind when you think of a clone? Personally, I see a bunch of little figures that all look the same and say, believe, and do the same things. If you were to peek inside a classroom, you'd see all of the little children sitting at cute little desks arranged in neat little rows. And while they're there, they all do what they're told, only speak when spoken to, and wouldn't dare to be different. Clone enough for you?

So what, in fact, are our children being taught while they're attending school? They're being taught to conform of course! Actually, I'd argue that conformity has become the goal of the educational system rather than providing education!

Remember the words that we, now grown-ups, heard repeatedly as we progressed through the educational system as children? Let me play back some of those tapes to refresh your memory:

"Why is yours different than Johnny's and Sally's?"

"This is the way we do it here!"

"Shut up and do what you're told!"

"Don't rock the boat!"

"Be good little boys and girls!"

And then they somehow expected us to develop creativity!

With this kind of upbringing, I don't know how some go on to achieve great things while others don't. Maybe it's nurturing. Maybe it's the right mentor. Maybe it's just plain luck. To be honest, I don't have an answer for this one. All I know is that there's not enough room for creativity in education. And with no room for creativity, it's no wonder why so many prodigies never live up to their potential—

nobody's ever given the opportunity to accomplish anything but what they're assigned in class!

At the end of the day, the true, underlying message that permeates the learning environment is: Don't you dare step out of line, or else! And if a child does happen to step out of line in some way, shape, or form, they're faced with the following line: "Do you want to go to the principal's office?" Or, how many times have we heard, "I think we're going to have to speak with your parents"?

And what happens when someone steps out of line or is different than everyone else? Out come the labels:

"Sally is developmentally delayed."

"Johnny is developmentally challenged."

"Sally has ADHD."

"Johnny has special needs."

"There is something wrong with Sally!"

In our present school system, if you don't fit in, you're removed from the mainstream program and placed in a "special" class to address your supposed shortcomings. This even happens to those who are actually quite brilliant and get so bored that they can't help but act out. With this reality, the real message the kids get is that it's bad and wrong to be different or in some way unlike the others. They get the idea that they're abnormal, incapable, or dumb. And for the rest of their lives, they never recover from the ongoing, irreparable damage to their self-image and self-esteem.

Education

As an aside, some might argue that there is nothing preventing parents from placing their children in more integrative and supportive establishments. But what's our reality? It costs money to do that; we need wads of cash to get our children the right education if they're different! Did you really think that attending the right school was a possibility? Those schools are only for the fortunate few! It's all about who you know and how much money you have, not who you are and what you're capable of.

So, what is a kid supposed to do? With all of the ongoing pressure, control, and judgment and no refuge, kids get horribly hurt by their fate. The pain and suffering builds up so much inside that they need to find a release. And what's the result? They lash out! You wind up with a rash of suicides and school shootings—kids taking everything out on schoolmates, school staff, or themselves!

Everyone blames video games and the media for the violence that exists in our society today. Sure, they may not help, but they're not the only culprits; in the end, the education system plays a role too. And who's behind all of these systems and establishments? Who or what should we really blame for spewing out all of these troubled and broken children? Yep, you guessed it: Blame it on fast foods!

I tell you, Steve can't wait to hear your thoughts on everything! Be sure to let him know exactly what you think!

CHAPTER EIGHT

Law and Politics

Some see the law as a nuisance, preventing us from living freely. Some see it as a Godsend, keeping certain elements of our lives in check. And to others, laws are seen as indicators of the inherent problems within our society. Ultimately, one's opinion on the subject depends on where one sits in relation to the law at a certain point in time. But in my case, my slant on the law has always been the same: The law is corrupt!

In our courts of law, those who bring the most money to the table triumph the majority of the time, regardless of how culpable they are. We've all seen how easy it can be to fabricate evidence and make other things disappear when enough money is thrown at a problem. As a matter of fact, with the right amount of money, even people can be made to disappear…if you know what I mean. And we can't forget how easy it is to "grease the palms" of court officials to ensure that certain loopholes and technicalities serve to work in your favour. It's all sick!

In essence, this amounts to a situation where those who have the most money—people who are often the true criminals—have more rights than the victims. The injustice in our legal system is very real. And as far as I'm concerned, the whole thing has been faulty from the get-go. What I mean by this is the true meaning of the word "justice" has been lost.

To have the scales of justice put back into balance, here's what I propose we do: Once guilt is established beyond a reasonable doubt, the guilty party receives a punishment that matches their wrongdoing or the injustice of their actions. For example, if a person was to murder another person by shooting them in the head, justice would entail having the wrongdoer get shot in the head as punishment. In my opinion, anything short of this is not just because the price paid by the wrongdoer is not equal to the damage that they inflicted; in other words, treatment should be exactly the same in order for true justice to take place.

Now, what are the chances of this kind of justice being put into place? Slim to nil. Why? Because there are too many bleeding hearts out there that would consider true justice to be too harsh. And what's worse is our politicians are too weak to even think of proposing it. This is especially true since the majority of politicians are corrupt to their very core, making their reason for disagreement obvious: They wouldn't dare put themselves in a situation where they could be subject to those kinds of repercussions. Likewise, with politicians frequently in the back pockets of the conglomerates, there's no way they'd let stiffer laws like this take root—it'd hurt their pocketbooks too much!

As my last point on the law, given what often happens in courtrooms and behind the scenes, I have to pause and say the following: If I had to venture a guess, the word "lawyer" came about from a simple misspelling of the word "liar." Now, since I might need a lawyer in the future—and maybe even the near future—I'll say that this doesn't apply to all lawyers. But, let's be honest: This sentiment does accurately describe their collective failure to uphold our justice system.

With the above points in mind, now appears to be the perfect time to introduce the next topic of interest: Politics.

To start, don't you find it interesting how a lot of politicians are lawyers? Remember what I said about the word "lawyer" being misspelled? In the world of politics, what we have is a bunch of liars who are only out there to get ahead and further their cause. And what's their cause? To help their conglomerate supporters gain more control over everyone and everything!

Since it's the politicians who make the law, it would only make sense that laws are created to give certain people an advantage over others. Why? Because politicians have people to keep happy—remember, they wouldn't be there if it wasn't for the campaign funding that they received! Why else would the conglomerates fund a political campaign?! They do it so they can get away with bloody murder, both figuratively and literally! It's corruption at its finest! And guess what happens if a politician grows a conscience? Well, that person surely won't last long, either due to an assassination or otherwise!

It's no wonder why politicians are always squirming when the "dirty laundry" of one of their supporters gets out into the media: They're stuck having to do what is necessary to make things go away! And to add insult to the imbalance of power in our society, all of our major media outlets are run by the conglomerates in the first place. If they need to influence public opinion, what better route than the public's primary source of "reliable information"?!

Is there a solution to all of this? Well, the only way to rectify matters is for the populace to take charge. But, do we even stand a chance of a snowball in hell? Of course not! Why? Because the conglomerates are huge and they control everything! So, here we are, right back at square one. And what do you do when there's nothing you can do? Blame it on fast foods!

CHAPTER NINE

Religion

Talking about hell, when I first thought up the need to discuss religion, I wasn't too sure of how I could tie the subject to fast foods. Then, I asked myself: Why are there so many religions out there? After about two seconds of thought, the answer came to me: Because each and every one of us wants our own answers to life's questions.

If you made a list of all the religions out there, you'd find that there's one for almost every mindset that exists. In other words, there's a smorgasbord of choice—just have a look through the menu and you'll find one that's perfect for you! With a religion to meet any slant or view on God—or lack thereof, for that matter—isn't this like the menus that hang over our heads at fast-food restaurants? Chose the religion that's to your taste and you're on your way!

What's the origin of this menu-like selection of religions? Well, in certain respects, it can be attributed to a childlike, "give me everything I want" type of attitude—"if you don't give me what I'm looking for, then I'm going elsewhere to get it!" And what's the result of this attitude? You get a bunch of religious establishments focusing solely on meeting the desires of their congregations, not doing what should be done to promote good in this world.

Too many people go around believing that "the self" is the "God" in their lives; the pride that people have in themselves is so large that it often becomes their belief system! It's the "holier than thou" type of view on things. The "I'm right and you're wrong" attitude. With so many people holding on to this type of value system, it causes many to be excluded, ostracized, and hurt. And what do people do when they feel that way? They reciprocate the same actions and blame the other party for initiating the behavior. The cycle never ends!

In extreme cases, some people can become so consumed by their own personal beliefs that they think they're God—the sole holders of the truth. In turn, they go about trying to coax others into believing that they're almighty and know the answers to all of life's questions. What's worse is they can become quite convincing. And then, what do you wind up with? A Jonestown massacre! If you haven't heard about it, look it up!

For those of you who don't like what I've said, my response is the following: The Devil made me do it! I have to shed responsibility and place the blame on someone else. On one hand, I don't want to burden anyone else—someone who lives and breathes as I do—with my shortcomings. On the other hand, there's no way in hell I'm going to take responsibility for my actions! So, as others do, I'm going to place my locus of control in the hands of God and The Devil. That way, when I do something good, I can take credit for being a suitable vesicle from which God does his handiwork, and when I do something inappropriate or wrong, it isn't my fault because I couldn't help but succumb to The Devil's powerful control! Convenient, isn't it?

To change gears, think about the following quote: "Hell is the realization of the reality of our misguided actions and consequences thereof." Kind of deep, isn't it? I just thought I'd include it in a vain attempt to make a point. And by the way, it didn't come from me; you can blame Steve for that one. I don't know where he got it from. Maybe he's just smarter than me.

Religion

Anyway, here's my slant on the quote: Different religions offer us different explanations as to the location of hell and what it is. In most cases, hell is punitive in nature. This leads people to shy away from or become more drawn to religion for fear of the punishment they could face for their actions or inaction. In other words, assuming responsibility scares the bejeebees out of people! So, how do they deal with this fear? Some choose not to believe in anything, and others become blinded by their religion.

Now, before I sign off and complete my critique of the subject, I feel obliged to present you with some pointed, concluding thoughts…

Since the beginning of time, many have had trouble with religion. Some of you may think that those folks are dumb, full of themselves, prideful, full of crap, crazy, or some combination of these. But, to them, their stance on religion is quite simple: religion = violence. Yes, **religion = violence**.

Stopping to consider this thought, how many wars have there been in the name of religion? How many men, women, and children have been killed in the name of God? Want some proof? Look to your daily news! Look through the history books! Look at The Bible! Look at yourself!

Think about it: I'd be willing to bet that the wide majority of those who read this would offer up and sacrifice their lives in the name of their belief system or religion. This has been going on since the very dawn of mankind—or "people-kind" if you find "mankind" sexist. And if you argue that you wouldn't even dare raise a hand to harm the smallest of hairs on someone else's head, I have one word for you: **Bull**! There's no doubt in my mind that a whole bunch of you would sacrifice your lives just to be remembered as a martyr. That's pride in full bloom!

You may be thinking: "Who is he to judge?!" Well, before you judge me—and neat how I turned this back on you—think about this: Maybe I'm the second coming of Jesus Christ. Oh the blasphemy! I kid, I kid…

Coming back down to earth, I'll be the first one to admit: I'm not perfect and neither is anyone else. And really, there is no way for us to truly know what is in the hearts and minds of others. Sure, we can have an idea after witnessing someone's actions, but some people can really put on an act! Anyway, all I mean to say is that people should start thinking for themselves and not only of themselves. Simple as that!

Out of pride—and boy does this word come up often—I won't take credit for all of the thoughts passed on within this chapter; much of what I've put together on religion is based on ideas offered by great people. Likewise, I don't profess to know it all…just most of it. And for everything that I don't know, and those who are quick to judge me, I blame it on fast foods!

CHAPTER TEN

Health

Over the span of our lives, we spend a large portion of our time getting beaten up, both mentally and physically. As a matter of fact, for many of us, we face this abuse each and every day. And sometimes, this mistreatment weakens us to the point where we become susceptible to persuasion and manipulation. Here's where the conglomerates come in…

Knowing how weak we can get, the conglomerates created fast food shacks to "feed the need" and "fill the void." They use their advertisements to try to create and entrench addiction, filling them with subliminal messages to convince us that we can't live without their junk. And they sacrifice our mental and physical well-being just to make a quick buck. Nice people, aren't they?!

No, the conglomerates surely don't care about us; all they want is for us to consume their trash and fill their pockets. But, maybe it's more complex than that. Maybe they don't really care about fulfilling our wants and needs. Maybe what they're actually trying to do is to make us even more ill! You know that the rich only want to get richer, right? Well, maybe they're working with the wealthy people of the "health industry" to get us all sick and make them rich! Think about how much money there is in private health and pharmaceuticals. It's a possibility, isn't it?

For example, consider the "healthy" fast-food options. The conglomerates claim that if you eat this food, you'll be healthy and lose weight. But, what are you really putting into your system? With one food, you'll cut out the sugar. With another, you'll cut down on the fat. And if you can cut out both, the "health food" is processed up the wazoo and isn't any better for you. Rarely can you ever find a fast food that is 100% healthy. If you do find one, it's either offered as part of a combo with some other junk—soda, chips, and the like—or it's extremely over-priced. You see what I mean? They try to get you any which way they can!

There's too much money involved for the conglomerates to stop doing everything in their power to promote sickness. Yes, you heard me right: <u>promote sickness</u>. You see, the more conglomerates make us sick, the more opportunities they have to "cure" us. It's a self-perpetuating cycle that churns out money for the health system. Even the government is involved so they can get a slice of the pie. It's a doozy of an opportunity for everyone involved!

Now, what is it that allows me to conjure up such a massive conspiracy? Not to hurt anyone's feelings, but consider cancer as an example. All of the so-called medical experts say that they know best how to treat cancer, yet the conventional methods of treating patients involve poisoning them. On top of that, if anyone even suggests an alternative or natural treatment, they're portrayed in the medical world as a quack. So, in the end, who gets all of the research grants to find a cure? Those who are part of the establishment of course! And what happens if someone does some research using their own funding? The health industry slams down the hammer and brings in the government and legal authorities. It's their way or the highway! The whole situation is sick—and yes, pun intended!

What can you or I do to change things? To be frank, nothing! If the conspiracy exists and it's as big as it could be, they have all the money and power to stop us! So, what are you left to do? That's right: Blame it on fast foods!

CHAPTER ELEVEN

"The Self"

In the course of our comings and goings, we all accumulate our own baggage. What I mean by this is our educational background and the ways in which we were parented and socialized have a significant impact on how we perceive ourselves and others. Likewise, we mustn't forget the biological predispositions that we've all inherited and how they can positively or negatively affect how we behave. Furthermore, there's the interplay between those predispositions, where certain character traits turn out asserting their dominance over others. And after combining this hodgepodge of influences, "the self" comes into being.

What do fast-food restaurants have to do with "the self"? Well, consider what drives people to go to fast-food joints in the first place: At a fast food restaurant, you can get what **you** want when **you** want it, no work or waiting period involved. What ever happened to the principles of working for what you get and having to wait for something good?

I'm sure many would argue that they toiled hard to earn the money to purchase what they want, and fast food is just a small reward for all of their work. But, as far as I'm concerned, I can think of much better things to soak my money into; a greasy, fat-filled burger, deep-fried fries, and a sugar-laden soda is not my idea of a reward! The truth is fast food is nothing but the proverbial nail driven into the cover of one's coffin. Get what I'm saying?

I bet that there are plenty more who say, "I, as an individual, am going to do what pleases me, and you can't do anything about it!" But if you stop and think about this statement, what are these people *really* saying? Everyone should simply stand back and let them kill themselves slowly? Sure, will do!

Simply put, people tend to think in the following terms: "How does _____ affect me?" In other words, "the self" is always at the center of all matters—self-conceit, self-pity, self-gratification, self-seeking, pride, and greed. Let's pursue each of these further, starting with self-conceit...

To paint the picture for you, consider some terms that are used to describe self-conceit, like "vain" and "egotistical." What do these words make you think of? Personally, what comes to my mind is how people can care so much about themselves and so little about others that they let everyone else suffer as they tend to their self. Just think of your experience with fast-food restaurants: How often do you see people butt in front of others to get served when it's not their turn? People step on each other left, right, and center to get to the front of the line! You see what I mean?!

Moving on to self-pity, think about how often you hear people say things like: "All of the cards are stacked against me!" I'm referring to the "poor little old me" syndrome— oh, the pain and injustice that life throws at us! Countless people hold this line of thought, believing that the world owes them everything and that anyone who gets in their way should be eliminated. It's the "better him/her than me" frame of mind. And even worse, they think that those who get eliminated deserve it. As far as I'm concerned, it's the ultimate form of selfishness!

Then we have self-gratification and self-seeking. In certain respects, we're talking about the same thing but from different perspectives. What I'm referring to is the behavior that comes out of such lines of thought—more of the "me first" kind of stuff. It's what leads people to pursue things that have an immediate return. It's the want for that which is instantaneous. It can be likened to the "instant" in instant coffee, instant rice, instant soup, and so on; it's the "fast" in fast food. It's no wonder why fast-food joints are so popular: They fulfill our presenting needs instantaneously!

And then there are the many who turn the finger on themselves. They are so obsessed with their guilt and culpability that they become depressed to the extreme. They hate and blame themselves mercilessly and incessantly for being the instruments of destruction in their own lives. And then there's the magazines, newspapers, and television programs that reinforce the idea that there is no hope. Fantastic, isn't it?!

What does this cause people to do? They cut themselves off from others. They dwell on the negative. They believe that they are powerless to influence their own lives. They turn into hypochondriacs. And then they take copious amounts of drugs to cure their ailments and stop the pain. It's no wonder why you get suicidal/homicidal maniacs so obsessed with ridding themselves of the pain that they go to fast-food restaurants and blow everyone away!

Come to think of it, maybe a more appropriate title for this chapter would have been "Selfishness." People nowadays have this "I deserve everything I want" type of attitude. Everyone is so consumed by "the self" and fulfilling their individual needs that they forget about everyone else.

Where does this mindset come from? Who's to blame for all of this selfishness? You know the culprit: Blame it on fast foods!

CHAPTER TWELVE

Relationships

Having just spoken about "the self," this appears to be the best time to introduce a subject that is close to us all: Relationships. But before we delve into the topic, let's stop and take a look at the meaning of the word…

As per its definition, a "relationship" is: "an affinity for or alliance with another person." Now, I'm not going to debate whether homosexual/lesbian unions qualify or should be excluded from any discussion on the subject. Instead, I'd like to remind you all that relationships do not need to be sexual in nature to qualify as such; friendships/unions of people of the same or opposite sex are still relationships!

With that aside, I'd like to start the discussion by asking you the following: What are relationships like in the real world? Does the definition above accurately describe how relationships usually function?

As I mentioned in the previous chapter, each and every one of us accumulates baggage over the span of our lives. Over time, this baggage often builds up to the point where we become hurting beings focused solely on ridding ourselves of the troubles that we possess. So, in turn, we wind up bringing these problems to the forefront of every relationship we have and do everything in our power to pass them off to whomever we can; in other words, hurt people hurt people!

Meanwhile, as we're trying to rid ourselves of our baggage, we try just as hard to fill the resulting void with something—or anything, for that matter. So, with each new relationship, we do everything in our power to siphon off whatever we can from the other party. As we do this, we fool ourselves into thinking that we're filling our void with something good, but oftentimes it's just someone else's issues—you know the saying, "one person's trash is another person's treasure"! Consequently, what you get is two beings playing musical chairs with their baggage. They haven't got a hope in the world of satisfying themselves, much less each other!

Considering this reality, it's not surprising that the divorce rate has passed the 50% mark and continues to rise each and every day. Some say that there's a cyclical nature to these statistics and that it will end at this point. Cyclical? Sure. But ends at this point? Bologna! People who get divorced nowadays often turn around and get hitched again right away—the whole cycle repeats itself ad nauseam!

Now that we've discussed the so-called adults, what about the children who are influenced by these toxic relationships? If you think that it's only a rollercoaster for the parents, think again—it's the children who bear the brunt of it!

Where do children go to fulfill their need for stability, security, and well-being? Moving from one home to the next, these poor souls keep getting uprooted while their parents search for "true love." But, throughout the process, their parents see nothing. Instead, they're focused on trying to fill what they perceive as a void in their life; they're focused on trying to fill the empty vesicle that they've become! However, as I spoke of earlier, all they're really doing is adding even more garbage to an already-filled, trash-infested container—and all at the expense of their kids! It's no wonder why these children grow up and repeat the cycle—talk about déjà-vu!

Blame it on fast foods

At this point, I'd like to throw something else into the pot: What about power and control? Does this not play a significant role in relationships? Well, of course it does! All of us are hungry for more power and control. These two items very quickly become the crux of every relationship, with one person always trying to gain the upper hand.

Once a position of dominance is established in a relationship, the individual with the upper hand never ceases in their attempt to gain more power. Instead, they continue to pick at the weaker party, like a parasite eats away at its host, until their partner is left bare and dry. And once that's complete, the vulture moves on to feast on its next carcass, picking at it until it too has nothing left to offer.

In relationships, there's always one person left as a hurting, empty unit, wondering what just happened, while the other is gorged with what they've taken from the other. When this is paired with the competitiveness that we're taught both at school and in the home, it's no wonder why so many people are out to get the better of each other!

To continue with my tirade, let's discuss what happens after a relationship has dissolved, specifically from a male's perspective on the situation...

Oftentimes, in the traditional male-female marriage, the woman may have sacrificed herself and her career by remaining in the home to care for the couple's offspring. Once such a relationship is severed, the man must then fulfill his responsibility toward the children by paying his fair share for their care. However, in typical cases of divorce, the scales are unfairly tilted in favour of women, even if they're employed outside of the home.

Relationships

What I mean is after a divorce, the male still pays the same share and the woman gets to add to it what she's raking in from her work. To me, this is like quitting a job and expecting to keep getting paid years after your departure. It doesn't make sense, but it happens every day!

Now don't get me wrong, there are those deadbeat fathers who have reneged on doing their part and should be dealt with in a stern manner. But who I'm referring to are those men who don't shirk their responsibilities and are taken advantage of by both women and the legal system. Simply put, there is a definite disparity and it's the men who often pay the price!

I'm sure that a lot of you think that what I've just said is sexist. As my rebuttal, consider a newspaper headline that I came across years ago: "We spend more time saving whales than males." Nowadays, this statement is so true!

Although our view on women has evolved—where they're equally considered as providers—we still haven't evolved to consider men as being equally capable nurturers. There are countless men who lose custody of their children because of the skewed view society has regarding a man's ability to care for children. And to boot, some women make it even worse and torture their ex-husbands by preventing them from ever seeing their children. It's horrible!

It's about time that the pendulum comes to justly sit somewhere in the middle. However, the women will never admit this because their present situation works to their own benefit. Disagree with me? Tell Steve!

And finally, there's the pride in relationships. How many times have we faced situations where another has wronged us or hurt us in some way, shape, or form? Naturally, we tend to take offense to it and hold a grudge, withholding our understanding and forgiveness to keep the other in our debt. In turn, this soothes our injured feelings and, even better, leads to contention...and we all love opportunities to pick fights and argue!

But with all of the fighting that's spurred from pride comes all sorts of costs. Picture these scenarios:

The wife is furious with the husband, so she starts throwing fine china or goes after him with a rolling pin. She is so upset that she wants to inflict the most pain possible!

Now, the husband, he chooses more expensive things to destroy. He'll put a golf club through the television or throw the sound system out the window. Then he'll put his fist through the wall or kick a dent in the refrigerator, in turn breaking a knuckle or foot, increasing the amount of pain he's feeling, and forcing him to go to the doctor to get some repairs. So, on top of the costs associated with repairing or replacing what he broke, if he doesn't have a good medical plan, he'll have to pay through the nose to repair himself!

In either case, all of this happened for what? Because someone left a spoon in the sink? Because someone left the toilet seat up? Come on!

In almost every fight, one person will blame the other for escalating the situation. But if we are, by chance, at fault for something and we know it, we will never admit it. Instead, we become defensive to justify our actions and protect our egos—it's easier that way! In essence, everyone already does what I recommend we all do: Blame it on fast foods!

CHAPTER THIRTEEN

Communication

To open this chapter, I say, "'Communication'? What 'communication?!'" The reality is that communication is a rare commodity in this world!

If you take a closer look at the word "communication," you'll find that its definition is a little misleading. What "communication" suggests is that there's a process whereby a message is passed from a sender to a receiver and that following the exchange, both parties possess the message. Also, after this action has taken place, the receiver's responsibility is to make a comment or gesture to indicate understanding of or agreement/disagreement with the conveyed message. Now, this comes under the assumption that the original message was tailored to meet the circumstance, the people involved, and that it was, in fact, understood. And only after all of these events is the process of "communicating" complete, allowing the whole affair to reach a point of closure.

As a concept, all of this sounds great. But, is this usually how communication takes place in the real world? I think not! It's no wonder why the term is often confused!

Based on what I see in most homes and workplaces, it truly seems as though most of this so-called communication is actually one-way conversation—there isn't much communicating going on if each person is acting as a dictator! Really, the messages that are transmitted to others often suggest that verbal or written discourse is non-participatory; people go about *telling* others what they have on their minds with no intention of accepting anything in return.

Blame it on fast foods

So, what message is really being sent? It's rather simple: "It's my way or the highway!" People are more sly than forthright about their true intentions. They prefer to hide everything for fear that the item being communicated will be misunderstood, dispelled, or simply disregarded. But they'll never admit this to others, much less to themselves. This is the insidious nature of communication in society today!

Consider the greetings people offer to others: One person says, "Hey! How's it goin'?" In return, the other replies with, "alright" or "pretty good." But is the initial greeting really an invitation to converse? And how about the reply—are they really putting in an effort to answer the question that was asked? And even further, consider the body language associated with this interaction: Both parties say these lines in passing, not even stopping to allow a real conversation to take place. This is precisely why I enjoy responding to questions of "How's it goin'?" with "Can't complain—no one is listening!"

Now, what is the root cause of this type of interaction (or lack thereof)? In response to this question, many would venture to say that people are just busy, in a rush, and that they don't have the time necessary to pursue a conversation. Others would say that people are being polite but short, so as to not take up the other's valuable time. But is any of this the truth, or are these just convenient excuses to get out of talking to anyone?

People in large cities have the best approach to communication that exists today: City folk do a lot of their communicating through gestures. As an example of this, consider the film "The Beverly Hillbillies."

Communication

In the movie, the Clampetts—a backwards-living, rural family—move to Beverly Hills to start a new life after striking rich. And when they arrive, how are they greeted? With "the finger." Not knowing any better—since they're "less civilized"—they interpret this gesture as a mode of greeting used by the locals and respond in the same fashion. As far as I'm concerned, they had the right idea!

I guess the point I'm trying to make is that although gestures do have their place in many situations, I fail to understand how they can become as common a form of communication as they are in urban centers today. So, the question is: Is it better to be greeted with "the finger" rather than not greeted at all? I'll leave you to decide that one for yourself.

At this point, I'm going to make a bit of a shift. As you read on, just stay with me—the link to communication will become apparent. Here we go!

The fast-food industry has infiltrated the world of computers. What makes me say this? Well, consider the quest for faster processors—again, we have this need to have things happen instantly. But with this quest to design computers that automate tasks and make our lives easier, we seem to have turned into computers ourselves!

What's really happened is we've become without senses, without feelings. Our computer-like lives have rendered us faceless and artificial. Like computers, if something doesn't quite compute, we discard it as impractical or impossible. In many respects, it's as if we've done this to separate ourselves from the real world; we've put up a layer of artificiality that acts as a barrier between ourselves and others.

Blame it on fast foods

But what does this all have to do with communication? Well, have you ever tried to talk to a computer? As you know, if you input something that the computer doesn't like, it sends you back an error message suggesting that you're out of sync or odd and responsible for the miscommunication. And yes, I know there are computers out there that can respond, but you know what I mean: There's nothing of substance inside that machine!

Now, consider all of the phone calls you've made to large companies or, even worse, government call centers. Every time, you face one of three situations: 1. You can't connect with whomever you're trying to reach; 2. The "service" is automated and doesn't offer any way to speak with a real human; or 3. If you can speak with a human, their scope of knowledge is so narrow that they freeze whenever you ask them anything challenging.

Thinking more about situation #3, it very accurately describes human interaction today. Nowadays, people have become machine-like with an objective rationale that is void of any feelings. You try to get help from someone and the "know it all" who's supposed to help winds up turning things on you so you feel like you've done something wrong. That or they don't even make an attempt to understand and simply reject what you're trying to convey. In the end, it's no different than "communicating" with a computer, receiving an error message no matter what you do. This makes communication quite difficult, if not impossible!

If the truth is that we're all good people at heart and we've simply become so busy that we can't stop to have a full conversation, then what has caused this? Is it the constant demands made on us by our work? Is it the demands placed on us by our families? Is it a result of our frequent use of technology?

Think about what texting/instant messaging has done to us. Today, you see the majority of people with their faces down, staring at the screen of their mobile device. They get so consumed by technology that they're oblivious to what is happening around them. Think about how many accidents have been caused by these distracted individuals as they thumb away at their machines and fail to communicate with their surroundings. Am I not correct when I say that there's something wrong with this picture?

As I suggested earlier, machines are separating us from the world under the guise of better communication. They insulate us from everyone and everything around us, making our lives completely artificial. And to those of you who argue that things like text messaging are communication, once again, I say, "Bologna!"

As far as I'm concerned, of all the influences discussed within this chapter, none of them are the true cause of our lack of communication. Instead, I think we should point to—or rather, flip off—the people who are really behind this issue: Blame it on fast foods!

CHAPTER FOURTEEN

Romance and Sex (the act)

In this day and age, we hear so much about how romance is dead. But is it really dead, or has the fast food mentality taken over one of the most intimate facets of our lives? Let's take a closer look...

First, what is romance? Well, after consulting the dictionary for accuracy, I couldn't believe what I had found: The word "romance" is spoken of as if it's fictitious, exaggerated, and without real substance rather than something of normal everyday life! And given this definition, everything became clearer: It's no wonder why people look for more romance in their lives—if my life sucked, I'd want to live in a fantasy world too!

To put things plainly, many people trick themselves into seeing their "romantic lives" as being better than they actually are. Instead of being productive and looking for a good and sustainable relationship, they do everything in their power to shelter themselves and protect the fantasy that they've created. Few come to realize that the life they're living isn't satisfying and, in turn, make a change. And the few who do make a change, like clockwork, turn out choosing a partner who's just as unsatisfying as the last one and create a new fantasy world no better than the one before.

How often do you hear people complain about who they're with and, instead of doing something about it, stay put and become miserable? Even though they're the ones to blame for their situation, they take out their frustrations on their partners. They start having "headaches" and feeling "sick," making them too tired to "perform." Nothing but a bunch of whiners!

Romance and Sex (the act)

And that's another thing that bugs the heck out of me: Why is it that a person has to "perform" in the first place? If it's supposed to be a performance, why not do it on a stage somewhere, in front of an audience?! It's no wonder why so many people in our society are sexually frustrated!

On the other side of things, some people go a little too far in making their fantasies a reality. This leads to some really sick kinds of stuff—stuff like sadism and masochism. Stuff like kiddy porn. And things like "snuff"—and no, I don't mean the stuff you put between your cheek and gums!

The point I'm trying to make is that on one hand, you have fantasies that are harmless and don't hurt anyone...beyond minor repairs, that is. And on the other hand, you have fantasies that, if acted out, can scar people for life or actually lead to death!

To start, you have sadism and masochism. If you're wondering where the heck this stuff came from, the answer to your question is simple: Some people have a perverse need to dominate or be dominated. It comes back to the power and control thing: Those who are powerless in their daily lives want to live out their fantasies of power and domination in the bedroom. Similarly, for those who actually do hold power, they're interested in finding out what it's like to be on the other side of things. And what's the result in both cases? You wind up with a bunch of people playing around with whips and chains. Now, isn't that good, wholesome fun!

In certain respects, I can understand what makes the concepts above appealing to some. But for the folks who love nothing but inflicting or receiving pain, I really can't understand them. I don't know about you people, but I try to experience the least amount of pain possible!

Then you have the most extreme version of disturbed pleasure out there, known universally by the term "snuff." "Snuff" involves torturing and mutilating an individual to death as a means of stimulating or attaining sexual gratification. In other words, people actually "get off" on that kind of stuff! If you don't believe me, look it up for yourself! It's revolting!

What happened to these people for them to behave in such a way? Were they dropped on their heads as babies or what?! That has to be it! Otherwise, maybe it's just what they were exposed to as they were growing up; maybe it's all they know. But although these may be reasons, they can't be used as excuses for this behavior. What these people really need is some therapy, that or some heavy-duty drugs to suppress these sick thoughts!

To bring things back in and return to normalcy, most of us consider romance to be the no kids, soft music, flowers, and candlelit dinner type of thing. And you have to admit, it sure is nice to slow things down and get intimate. As they say, "it helps us 'get in the mood.'"

But do you expect this kind of treatment all of the time? Odds are your immediate response is a "no." In most relationships, the flame tends to only last for a little while before it turns out being "too much work." All the same, deep down inside, most of us would love to have this type of "soirée" on a regular basis, regardless of how unrealistic it would be to do so.

Romance and Sex (the act)

Now, instead of a romantic evenings at home, what usually takes place behind closed doors? Nowadays, it's more along the lines of: "wham, bam, thank you ma'am (or man)!" With all of the romantic nights that we don't make time for, people wind up having so much pent-up sexual energy that they become self-centered and desperate for a release.

Given this reality, what quickly becomes the root mindset behind our sexual behavior? Is it self-gratification? Self-centeredness? To me, it's both! It's no wonder why so many people cheat, use, and abuse! Pretty callous, isn't it?

These days, so many people are focused solely on "getting off" and don't even recognize that there's another person present. They're only interested in achieving their climax and that's it! Then, at the end of it all, what happens when one climaxes and the other doesn't? The one who didn't climax gets down, depressed, and "turns off." And where does that leave the two of them? Right back where they started: uninterested, distant, and alone.

A lot of people expect sex at the snap of their fingers; they expect sex whenever they want it, wherever they want it, and however they want it. And what happens if you can't satisfy their needs? They'll go find someone else who can! It's all about a quick "in and out"!

What does all of this "romance" remind you of? You know the answer: The fast food industry! So, what should you do when you're not getting any loving and your sex life has gone to hell? Blame it on fast foods!

CHAPTER FIFTEEN

Parenting and Socialization

The fast-food mentality has crept into one of the most important and sacred realms of human existence: The home. But, how has it affected life at home? Well, it's simple...

The whole process starts when parents make the decision to have a child. Some say that a child is born out of love and a desire to achieve immortality by extending one's bloodlines. Others say that a child is a blessing that must be protected and nurtured. If you believe that the latter is the case, look back to some of the points I made about how kids are treated. Do you honestly believe that parents protect and nurture their children?

From what I see, most parents seem to think their job is to raise their children quickly so they can get them out of the house as soon as possible. That way, the parents can actually get on with their lives. In fact, parents take no time at all to get their infants out of the home. Don't believe me? Look no further than the lucrative business of daycare.

It makes you wonder if parents say to each other, "After we have a kid, let's quickly hand over the responsibility of caring for and raising the child to someone else!" If you ask them if that's the case, what's their typical excuse? Poor mom and dad need to get back to work so they can earn enough money to take care of their child. But what are they really doing? As far as I'm concerned, they're doing their absolute best to get out of the chore of child-rearing. It's too hard and time-consuming! Why not let the experts do it?! Having others take care of the job is the best "bang for your buck"!

Parenting and Socialization

Yes, the going excuse nowadays is that the parents only want what's best for their children. And many would suggest that I should take into consideration the effort taken by parents to find the best childcare facility available. But honestly, don't kid yourself—parents are simply trying to renege on their responsibilities. If you don't agree with me, consider this...

If a parent winds up with a psychotic, serial-killer teenager (or adult), they're quick to blame it on television, music, or other influences that are omnipresent in our lives. The parents cry out: "It's society's fault!" "We are not to blame!" "We did our best!" Convenient approach, isn't it? So, parents start by reneging on their responsibility for their children, and then when something runs amuck, they blame it on someone or something else! In other words, people throw the kid into someone else's hands so they don't have to assume any responsibility! Well done!

But all of this is talking about things from a parent's perspective. What about the kids? What happens to the children in the process? I hinted at it when I made my comment about psycho teenage/adult serial-killers, but let's delve into things a little further...

How are kids treated in our society today? They're treated as commodities. And I know what you're thinking: "How dare you say such a thing?!" But consider this: Children belong to their parents. How many times have we heard things to that effect? Statements like: "These are my children." "They belong to me." "They're mine!" To put it plainly, children are viewed as just another one of their parents' possessions!

Blame it on fast foods

This sentiment is especially apparent in cases of divorce. Think about how often you hear of custodial battles. And on that note, consider the definition of the word "custody"—it includes statements like "for keeping," "restraint of liberty," "confinement," and "imprisonment." Our children are being abused! They're no different than prisoners of war!

Some say that the home is supposed to be a safe haven for our children. But is the home really a safe place?

As a matter of fact, it turns out that the home is one of the most dangerous places to be. Without any outlets to release the frustrations that accumulate from functioning in the hustle-and-bustle world that they live in, parents can't hold themselves back from striking out at their children. Actually, I'd argue that parents do more "surviving" than "functioning" in the real world with all the injustices they have to endure. It's no wonder why negative emotions are passed on to or taken out on our children!

So, now what are we left with? What is the aftermath of all the strife and subsequent problems that people must endure? Simply put, we are left with a society made up of victims: There are victims of wife abuse, husband abuse. There are victims of parental abuse and abuse of the elderly. There are victims of love and sexual assault. And there are also victims of indifference.

No one comes out of things unscathed; we all have our own crosses to bear. This victimization leads many to point the finger outwards. And sure, why not see yourself as powerless? That way, you don't have to do anything about it but lay the blame on someone or something else!

Parenting and Socialization

At this point, I'm torn over the idea of adding some levity to my discourse. Is there really anything to laugh about when it comes to the wellbeing of children? Well, maybe there is...

Think about the instances when an adult speaks to a baby. Can you hear their tone of voice? The animated, high-pitched and incessant baby-talk? Now picture the faces of the child and the adult: The grin of the adult. The wide-eyed gaze of the child and gurgling sounds that he/she makes. Now, consider the language the adult uses: the "goo-goo-gah-gah" kind of stuff. There's nothing more powerful on this earth than an infant's ability to turn an otherwise intelligent, well-adjusted adult into an incoherent, babbling idiot! I hope that this thought puts a smile on your face!

Returning back to the topic at hand, stop and think about what I've suggested in this chapter. It's no wonder why parents shy away from the job of child-rearing and put the responsibility into someone else's hands. It's not unlike the proverbial catch-22; you're damned if you do because you can't do a good enough job, and you're damned if you don't because others can't get the job done either! In my view, what we're actually talking about is opening Pandora's Box—once a child "pops out," it's as if they are let loose on the world. Without proper parenting, kids turn out doing whatever they feel like. And since our children are products of the society we live in, in many respects, we should expect that our kids will portray all of the ills of the human race; in other words, the result is that things will often go wrong.

If any of the comments I've made have hurt you, I'm sorry—especially if you're someone who's wallowing in their own misery. And if sorry won't cut it, I have but one thing to say: Blame it on fast foods!

CHAPTER SIXTEEN

The End

To close my dissertation, I submit that fast food is the cause of all that's wrong in society today. Fast food makes us sick! Fast food ruins our lives! Fast food is the root of all evil! If fast food didn't exist, our world would be a better place!

And to recap, who's behind the fast-food industry? As I've explained in this book, it's the conglomerates! They have control over all of us and we don't even know it! Yes, I'm referring to a conspiracy!

I ask you: Are we, as separate entities, living a reality based on our own everyday perceptions, or are we actually products of a reality that is being imposed upon us? Most of us believe that we are in control of our own destinies, but this concept of "the self" is just a tool used by the conglomerates to divert our attention and disguise the truth.

The truth is that we, as a people, are nothing but hoards of followers, trying to fit in instead of living our own lives. Disagree? Look no further than the worlds of fashion and fame—there, everyone is following or hitching onto someone or something else.

What we've become is a colony of lemmings. In this colony, all of the lemmings look the same, think the same, and do the same things. And what's going to happen to this colony of lemmings? They'll become so consumed by the process of following each other's coattails that they all wind up falling off the edge of a cliff!

The End

You see, the title of this chapter is most appropriate—if we continue on as the lemmings we've become, succumbing to the control that the conglomerates have over us, maybe this is or will lead to the end of our existence!

If you're shaking in your boots at this point, wanting to offer a rebuttal to my disturbed train of thought, you're in luck—Steve would love to hear it! But not quite yet; you're going to have to wait a little longer. If this upsets you, know that I'm only trying to break the cycle of instant gratification that we've all gotten caught up in. Rest assured, you'll get his contact information in due time!

Yes, after reading all of these rants, thoughts, ramblings, and so on, you're most likely saying to yourself, "What a warped, twisted, bitter, and evil person!" And honestly, I'd probably have to agree with that sentiment! But, for my own sake, I'd rather see myself as a resilient and adaptable survivor. I abstain from fast foods and am healthier for it!

Now, what about you? What is your role in this whole mess? What are you going to do? Are you going to willingly participate in this tragedy and perpetuate the problem, or are you going to take a stand? Do something about it! Fight back! Don't let yourself get caught up in this insidious juggernaut!

Wait one second! Where do I get off turning things back on you again? You see, people are very quick to point the finger at others yet they don't even take a moment to look at themselves in the mirror!

Just as often, people place the blame on hard luck. They get upset by the hand that they were dealt. But, as far as I'm concerned, it's all in the perspective you take; it's all in the way you see things and what you do with what you have. You do have a choice in the matter. Don't crawl up in a ball and cry about your life! Take things in hand! Take yourself in hand! Make changes! It's time to put an end to this cycle of self-destruction!

Do you remember way back at the beginning of this book when I said that I wouldn't leave you with any gems of wisdom or pearls of great price? Well, I lied! Here's my advice: Take stock of your life; make an inventory of what you have, what you want and need, and consider the means to attain what you wish. Then, make a plan and do what is necessary to make it happen. And most importantly, don't forget to secure the help and support of others in the process. It's simple and it works if you put in an effort and do it!

And finally, I would like to leave you with my last little gem of wisdom...

If you think that life is unfair and you haven't been given a fair shake, all I can say to you is "Get over it!" And if, by chance, you can't get over it, then you're just going to have to get used to it. And if neither of the two work for you, do the only thing left that you can do: Blame it on fast foods!

Epilogue

Although this book was meant to present you with a satirical view of Western society, I hope that it has spawned some thought. It's time that we make some much-needed change before mankind implodes. We need to do something to get out of the hamster wheel. Enough is enough! And always remember that there is strength in numbers. If we all do this together, there is no stopping us!

And last, I guess I should keep my promise and leave you with a means to get a hold of Steve. If you do plan to message him, keep in mind that he's a busy guy and may not be able to respond right away. In any case, you can e-mail him at: BlameItOnSteveInstead@gmail.com. Be sure to let him know what you think…but, of course, be gentle!

About the Author

B. J. T. Pepin was born in East-Central Canada and was raised there alongside his three brothers.

After a couple years of post-secondary education, B. J. T. Pepin joined the Canadian Armed Forces. He began his service as a Non-Commissioned Member in the role of Avionics Technician. Within a few years, he was selected to receive university training and chose to pursue a career in Social Work. After completing his Bachelor of Social Work, he became an Officer and completed his Masters within his last 10 years of service. Altogether, his contribution equals 20 years as an Officer and 27 total years of service.

During those years of service, B. J. T. Pepin had two wonderful children—one boy and one girl. Both of his children are now grown up and he is fortunate enough to have two grandchildren.

B. J. T. Pepin remarried and has settled in East-Central Canada with his lovely wife…and his mutt of a dog.

CPSIA information can be obtained
at www.ICGtesting.com
Printed in the USA
BVHW032147131118
533088BV00001B/74/P

9 780988 105508